Walther Ziegler

Smith
in 60 Minutes

Translated by
Alexander Reynolds

My thanks go to Rudolf Aichner for his tireless critical editing; Silke Ruthenberg for the fine graphics; Lydia Pointvogl, Eva Amberger, Christiane Hüttner, and Dr. Martin Engler for their excellent work as manuscript readers and sub-editors; Prof. Guntram Knapp, who first inspired me with enthusiasm for philosophy; and Angela Schumitz, who handled in the most professional manner, as chief editorial reader, the production of both the German and the English editions of this series of books.

My special thanks go to my translator

Dr Alexander Reynolds.

Himself a philosopher, he not only translated the original German text into English with great care and precision but also, in passages where this was required in order to ensure clear understanding, supplemented this text with certain formulations adapted specifically to the needs of English-language readers.

Bibliographic Information held by the German National Library: The details of the original German edition of this publication are held by the German National Library as part of the German National Bibliography; detailed bibliographical data can be found online at www.dnb.de.

© 2016 Dr Walther Ziegler
1st Edition June 2016
Jacket design and graphic design for the whole book: Silke Ruthenberg, making use of illustrations by:
Raphael Bräsecke, Creactive – Studio for Advertising, Comics & Illustrations
© JackF - Fotolia.com (image-frames)
© Valerie Potapova - Fotolia.com (image-frames)
© Svetlana Gryankina - Fotolia.com (speech-balloons)

Publisher and Printing:
BoD – Books on Demand, Norderstedt
ISBN 9783741227653

Inhalt

Smith's Great Discovery	**7**
Smith's Central Idea	**12**
The Four Stages of History	12
The Division of Labour	22
Free Trade	28
The Free Play of Supply and Demand	36
The Invisible Hand	42
The Duties of the State	55
Taxes as an Instrument for Redistributing Wealth	61
Of What Use is Smith's Discovery for Us Today?	**64**
Smith's Great Vision – Prosperity for All!	64
The System of Natural Liberty – Smith's Warning Against the Planned Economy	70
Global Economic Crises – the End of the 'Invisible Hand'?	75
From "Night-Watchman State" to "Welfare State" – The Legacy of Adam Smith	81
Bibliographical References:	**87**

Smith's Great Discovery

It was, of all people, a Scottish philosopher of morality that became the intellectual forefather of capitalism. Adam Smith was the first to recognize and describe, in 1776, the basic principle of the market economy. His magnum opus, *The Wealth of Nations*, is still spoken of today as "the Bible of capitalism". And indeed, for a period of ten years it was, after the Bible itself, the most-translated book on earth.

Overnight, this nine-hundred-page work made Smith (1723-1790) the founder of a whole new science: "political economy", nowadays usually referred to just as "economics". In it he described for the first time the central mechanism of capitalism and created the "magic formula" of the free play of supply and demand. His theory of "the invisible hand" spread like wildfire around the world and remains still today the core of the capitalist market model.

But Smith did much more than just exactly describe the functioning of capitalism. He also provided philosophical reasons why the free-market economy is the best of all possible economic systems. His explanation is as simple as it is astounding. Each human being, he argues, is egoistic by nature; everybody aims, in the first instance, to achieve his or her own interests. The free-market economy concords with this all-too-human disposition – one might even say: this natural human drive – by giving everyone the chance to increase their wealth. But whoever, Smith goes on, works industriously to improve the quality of his own life in fact promotes, indirectly and without intending to, the good of society as a whole:

> By pursuing his own interest, he frequently promotes that of the society more effectually than when he really intends to promote it. [2]

Thus, argues Smith, the capitalist production process transforms, as if it were a process guided by an "invisible hand", the entrepreneur's egoistic concern for personal profit into something that benefits all. The many competing producers think, indeed, only of their own profit; but the sum of their actions ensures that there are always enough reasonably-priced goods on supermarket shelves. One achieves this simply by allowing economically active people a free hand. Smith thus called for the abolition of customs duties and guild restrictions, preparing the way for the economic liberalism that characterizes the global economy today:

> In general, if any branch of trade, or any division of labour, be advantageous to the public, the freer and more general the competition, it will always be the more so. ³

This championing of unlimited free competition is all the more astonishing given that Smith was born in Scotland as the son of a customs comptroller. But we see no trace in him either of the proverbial illiberality of the Scots or his father's profession. On the contrary, he was far ahead of his time in hoping that, once customs duties had been abolished, global free trade and unrestricted capitalist production would eventually ensure prosperity for all:

> It is the great multiplication of the productions of all the different arts [...] which occasions, in a well-governed society, that universal opulence which extends itself to the lowest ranks of the people. ⁴

Smith was the first to recognize the explosive power of industrialization. With his description and legitimation of capitalism he created a body of ideas that form the economic basis of the whole Western world. Even his critics recognize Smith's achievement here. Thus, the economist Joseph Schumpeter calls The Wealth of Nations "the most successful not only of all books on economics but, with the possible exception of Darwin's *Origin of Species*, of all scientific books that have appeared to this day." ⁵

Corporate bosses, high-level managers and top politicians usually know the book very well. Margaret Thatcher is said to have made reading all of it compulsory for all her cabinet ministers and to have checked in personal interviews that each minister had "done their homework". But, though economic policy-makers generally know Smith, everyone living in the market economy – and that, today, means almost everyone alive – really ought to be familiar with his basic ideas. The "invisible hand" mechanism and the "free play of supply and demand" are in fact more than just theories; they are the very heart of the capitalist world. Understanding them, then, is an imperative, since they form the economic and philosophical basis of the world in which we live and, in all probability, will continue to live all our lives.

Does the "invisible hand" really work? Does egoistic economic energy really tend to be transformed into social prosperity? May one, then, really leave the economy to take its course? Adam Smith gives convincing answers to these questions.

Smith's Central Idea

The Four Stages of History

Already in the introduction to *The Wealth of Nations* Smith makes implicit reference to his own ambitious idea of dividing the whole of human history into four succeeding ages: the age of hunters; that of shepherds; that of agriculture; and his own age of commerce and industry. But Smith understands the motor driving all these stages of history to be self-interest or, as he puts it, the striving for personal prosperity. This, he claims, is innate in Man and is Man's essential distinguishing feature: we are constantly driven by "the desire of bettering our condition":

[...] a desire which [...] comes with us from the womb, and never leaves us till we go into the grave. [6]

Smith, then, clearly states his basic belief that Man is essentially and entirely an egoist. But for Smith this is no bad thing but rather the source of all progress. Because, as he argues, "the pleasures of wealth and greatness [...] strike the imagination as something grand and beautiful and noble, of which the attainment is well worth all the toil and anxiety which we are so apt to bestow upon it."[7] Man thus runs great risks and makes great efforts with a view to gaining prosperity. And even if the pleasure of personal profit proves, in the end, not to be so great, the years of committed industriousness will have served, indirectly, to improve conditions of life for all:

And it is well that Nature imposes on us in this manner. It is this deception which rouses and keeps in continual motion the industry of mankind. It is this which first prompted them to cultivate the ground, to build

> houses, to found cities and commonwealths, and to invent and improve all the sciences and arts which ennoble and embellish human life, which have entirely changed the whole face of the globe, have turned the rude forests of Nature into agreeable and fertile plains, and made the trackless and barren ocean [...] the great high road of communication to the different nations of the earth.[8]

It is self-interest, then, that motivates historical progress and the global process of civilization. The first stage of development here is the age of hunters and gatherers. Human beings gain their livelihood by hunting or by gathering the fruits of the earth. In this era there is no property. Tribes work together to hunt down animals and share the results. Smith considers the American Indians who followed the buffalo herds across the Great Plains to be an example of a highly developed hunter culture. Accumulation of property was impossible here because each Indian could own no more than could be transported behind a horse from site to site. Hunter-gatherer society, therefore, displays great equality. In this stage of history there is not even a government, because:

> Where there is no property [...] civil government is not so necessary. [9]

The second great historical epoch is that of shepherds and cattle-breeders. Man has now discovered that it is easier to breed animals than hunt them in the wild. Livelihoods are now gained by animals' domestication. There thus arises property in the form of camels, sheep or cattle. But no true government comes into being as yet.

This we see for the first time in the next epoch: that of agriculture. The reason for this, says Smith, is that livelihoods are now gained by the planting of fields, so that tracts of land must now be fenced off. Property arises in the form of ownership of this land, which makes the landless totally and non-reciprocally dependent on the landowners. Life is now hard for those who own nothing.

The slaves, serfs and villeins who worked land held

by feudal tenure were not only materially dependent on their landlord, being bound to perform unpaid work for him; they were also forbidden to move elsewhere and even had to ask their lord's permission to marry. This one-sided dependency, argues Smith, led to a stagnation of production:

A person who can acquire no property can have no other interest but to eat as much and to labour as little as possible. [10]

Here too it is clear that Smith considers self-interest to be Man's strongest motive. Since Man is egoistic and always seeks his advantage, a slave or a serf will naturally work as little as possible. Working more would bring him nothing, since he must cede the whole harvest to the landlord anyway. This latter's accumulating riches also gives rise to ever greater resentment:

Smith's Central Idea

> The affluence of the rich excites the indignation of the poor, who are often both driven by want and prompted by envy to invade his possessions. [11]

Serfs and landless peasants also remain, during this stage of history, legally dependent, since their noble feudal lord is both legislator and judge. This feudal society is the first in history, then, to need a government and civil authorities because – so Smith argues – without these the inequality of this society could not be enforced:

> It is only under the shelter of the civil magistrate that the owner of that valuable property [...] can sleep a single night in security. [12]

Smith, then, sees the state – much as Marx did a century later – as, in its origin, a tool of the ruling classes used to maintain social inequality. But for Smith all this changes in the next stage of history.

There now occurs an unexpected turn in the history of mankind: namely, the transition to our modern industrial era. Smith speaks here of a revolutionary change: specifically, of "the great revolution". On the view defended by Smith there has really only been one true revolution: the Industrial Revolution. Because "revolution" comes from the Latin word revoluere, meaning "to turn around", "turn over" or "transform". And human life has in fact never, at any point in history, been so fundamentally transformed in so short a time as through the transition from agricultural to industrial society.

The modern industrial worker is no longer, as the peasant farmer had been, dependent on the seasons, or even on the rhythm of day and night. Thanks to canning and other preservative methods and new forms of transport, things can now be eaten all year round that could once only be eaten in specific seasons. Extended families are disintegrating. More and more people live in cities. But above all – and this, for Smith, is the decisive difference – people now gain their livelihoods by the exchange of commodities for money. This money comes either from some form of annuity, from invested capital, or from the sale of one's own labour.

The line between the "haves" and "have-nots" is no longer absolute. Because in industrial society even a man who owns no land or capital is at least the owner of his own labour-power. This he can sell competitively on the market. Smith celebrates this as a great historical gain:

The property which every man has in his own labour, as it is the original foundation of all other property, so it is the most sacred and inviolable. [13]

The factory workers as well as the agricultural workers are no longer bound, as in the Middle Ages, to a single piece of land, slaves to a feudal lord who maintains their lives with recompense "in kind". Rather, they can move about freely and even save from their wages to build up their own capital, emigrate to America, or open their own business. Such mobility, indeed, was still limited in Smith's day; but the one-sided dependency of feudal society was already beginning inexorably to give way to the "dependency of all on all" of the industrial age. The factory-owner is dependent on the workers who sell him their labour, the suppliers who provide raw materials, and on the wholesalers, retailers and consumers who, in the end, buy what he produces.

This mutual economic dependency that characterizes a developed market society leads, argues Smith, to greater personal freedom and, in the end, to equality before the law. Smith believed, as Marx did later, that a material change in the mode of production was always necessarily followed by a change in the political form of society. Not only the well-off bourgeoisie, prophesied Smith, but also ordinary workers would, sooner or later, due to their essential role in economic life, begin to press for political power and universal free elections. And within a hundred years this had indeed happened in most European countries. But most especially Smith saw the transition to industrial society as involving the shattering of the restraints of the old guild system. Formerly, the blacksmith's son was bound to become a blacksmith, the baker's son a baker, the serf's son a serf etc. But in modern society with its division of labour, Smith foretold, all these medieval guild restrictions would sooner or later be swept away. Here too he was proven right.

It must be borne in mind that Smith was writing at the very beginning of this Industrial Revolution. The first cotton mills and still quasi-artisanal factories had just begun to arise. The steam engine had been invented but there were, as yet, no railways. Nevertheless Smith recognized the tremendous explosive power of the new mode of production, seeing industrial society as the fourth and highest stage of human social development after the stages of hunter-gatherer, pastoral, and agricultural production. Only now, as a consequence of industrialization, was there a historical chance of an entire nation's, and eventually – such was Smith's great vision – of all mankind's, enjoying prosperity. It was not least for this reason that he entitled the book which brought him fame *The Wealth of Nations*.

The Division of Labour

One reason for Smith's optimistic prognosis was the emergence, in his lifetime, of the practice of the division of labour. To point up the enormous efficiency of the new industrial mode of production Smith uses his famous example of the pin-maker:

> A workman [...] could scarce, perhaps, with his utmost industry, make one pin in a day, and certainly could not make twenty. But in the way in which this business is now carried on [...] it is divided into a number of branches, of which the greater part are [...] peculiar trades. [14]

Whereas, formerly, a worker had formed and forged, alone, a single needle from beginning to end – setting the head on it himself and so on – he now takes on only a small part of the production process and passes his part-product on to other workers:

Smith's Central Idea

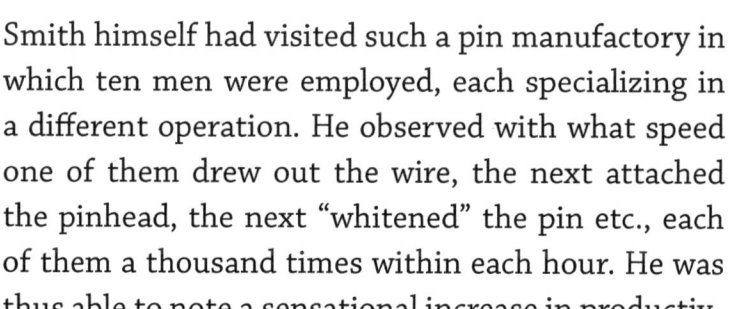

> One man draws out the wire, another straights, a third cuts it, a fourth points it, a fifth grinds it at the top for receiving the head; to make the head requires three distinct operations; to put it on is a peculiar business; to whiten the pins is another; it is even a trade by itself to put them into the paper [...]. [15]

Smith himself had visited such a pin manufactory in which ten men were employed, each specializing in a different operation. He observed with what speed one of them drew out the wire, the next attached the pinhead, the next "whitened" the pin etc., each of them a thousand times within each hour. He was thus able to note a sensational increase in productivity:

> Those ten persons, therefore, could make, among them, upward of forty-eight thousand pins in a day (or) each person [...] four thousand eight hundred pins [...].

> But if they had all wrought separately and independently [...] they could certainly not each of them have made twenty, perhaps not one pin in a day. [16]

In this case, then, the productivity of one man increases, due to specialization and the division of labour, almost fivehundredfold. Smith explains how the same occurs in the manufacture of clothing due to specialization in spinning, weaving, dying and tailoring. It becomes for the first time possible that the common folk no longer, as for many centuries before, goes clad in rags and hides but is rather supplied with a great choice of clothing by the textile industry. Differences in appearance between rich and poor, Smith foretold, would vanish as a result of industrialization. Here too he proved a prophet. Whoever walks about in a European metropolis today can indeed no longer tell, just by people's appearance, what income-class they belong to – something that would have been all too easy in antiquity, the Middle Ages, or even Smith's own era.

Smith's Central Idea

Division of labour, Smith explains, makes people in the industrial era closely mutually dependent on one another, since each performs only a single specialized activity and is able to make only a part of any given product. An architect, for example, can design houses all by himself but in order to do this effectively, he needs paper, pencils, rulers, clothes, food and personal transport made by other productive people. And once it comes to actually building the house he has designed, he needs an engineer to make the structural-engineering calculations and bricklayers, carpenters, roofers and electricians to execute his designs. Only animals, writes Smith, and perhaps the first prehistoric humans were truly individually self-sufficient, seeing to their shelter and nourishment each by himself:

In almost every other race of animals each individual, when it is grown up to maturity, is entirely independent [...]. But Man has almost constant occasion for the help of his brethren and it is vain for him to expect it from their benevolence only. [17]

Here too Smith reaffirms his image of Man as an egoist, guided primarily by self-love. Though dependent on the help of others, we cannot just rely for this on their benevolence and love of their fellow man. If we have a strong desire for tomatoes, but work in the city and have no vegetable garden of our own, we would be foolish to imagine that the farmer will give us them out of the kindness of his heart. That man is much more likely to achieve his desires who, instead of appealing to human empathy, pursues his interest by respecting the self-love of others and including this in his plans:

He will be more likely to prevail if he can interest their self-love in his favour, and show them that it is for their own advantage to do for him what he requires of them [...]. [18]

But how does one bring others to do "what one requires of them"? And how can it lie in the interest of someone else to do specifically what I require? Smith's answer is simple and convincing: money. If he is paid for it, every one of my fellow citizens, however egoistic, will have a definite interest in giving me what I need:

It is not from the benevolence of the butcher, the brewer or the baker that we expect our dinner but from their regard to their own interest. [19]

The fresher, crisper and more attractively priced the baker's rolls are, the more of them he will sell. It is not, then, the baker's fellow feeling but rather his self-love that prompts him to give of his best for our benefit.

Free Trade

Just because, then, it lies in every person's most basic and essential interest to make the products that he can make best and to exchange these for other products, division of labour and exchange of this sort are the source of all wealth and prosperity:

It is the maxim of every prudent master of a family never to attempt to make at home what it will cost him more to make than to buy. The tailor does not attempt to make his own shoes, but buys them of the shoemaker. The shoemaker does not attempt to make his own clothes [...]. [20]

The same applies to the other professions:

> The farmer attempts to make neither the one nor the other, but employs those different artificers. All of them find it for their interest to employ their whole industry in a way in which they have some advantage over their neighbours and to purchase with a part of its produce [...] whatever else they have occasion for. [21]

As a rule, division of labour is generally the most rewarding option. And this not only for individuals but also, Smith argues, for states:

> What is prudence in the conduct of every private family can hardly be folly in that of a great kingdom. [22]

If a commodity can be produced in one state better and more cheaply than it can in another, then one ought also to buy it in the former state. Senseless, therefore, are import duties and every sort of protectionistic policy adopted by national states. With these, states attempt to strengthen their own economies by stopping the import of foreign goods. But they achieve exactly the opposite. Such measures tend rather always to reduce one's own nation's prosperity. Adam Smith illustrates this by the example of English red wine.

It is in fact possible, with great effort, to cultivate grapes of the sort used for Burgundy wines even in the chilly British Isles. If one plants the vines directly up against a brick wall, the warmth absorbed by the wall on sunny days is released into the vines at evening. Alternatively, one can raise the vines in greenhouses, using large amounts of horse-dung as fertilizer.

But all this means, Smith points out, that the production of red wine in England requires some thirty times the expenditure of time and effort that would be involved in buying it from the French. It would make no sense at all, then, to keep French red wine out of the country by imposing high import duties with a view to protecting England's own wine production. Because even if such measures succeeded, English red wine would still be so expensive to produce that, for example, an English artisan who made pliers would have to sell some ten pairs of pliers in order, with the revenue, to acquire a single bottle of such wine.

As a rule, however, the same revenue from ten pairs of pliers would get this artisan some thirty bottles of French red wine. Furthermore, as a reaction to the duties imposed by the English on their wine, the French might for their part impose import duties on English pliers and, simply out of spite against England, increase their own manufacture of the tool in question, even though this would involve as disproportionate an effort for France as the making of wine for England, since France has no access to iron ore of the quality needed. The people of both nations, then, would end up, due to such mercantilist protective duties, having the same products but at thirty times the expenditure of labour. Both countries, in other words, would hereby, quite unnecessarily, have forfeited twenty-nine units of time during which they might have been producing other things that would have been much more conducive to their respective nation's welfare.

Smith thus called for global trade unburdened by

customs duties and was highly critical of these policies which we have called, above, "mercantilist". The mercantilists were, for the most part, ministers and counsellors to kings and advocated the view that the best way for a country to increase its own wealth was to support exports while preventing all imports, thus drawing into the country, or retaining within it, the greatest possible amount of gold and silver. Smith writes of this policy:

> Consumable commodities, it is said, are soon destroyed; whereas gold and silver are of a more durable nature and, were it not for this continual exportation, might be accumulated for ages together, to the incredible augmentation of the real wealth of the country. [23]

But Smith believed this to be an absurd line of reasoning. Because a state in fact needs only so many gold and silver coins as are really required for day-to-day currency circulation. Simply to store up such coins in dark storehouses would thus be quite useless. It would be as absurd as

Smith's Central Idea

> [...] to attempt to increase the good cheer of private families by obliging them to keep an unnecessary number of kitchen utensils. [24]

The wealth of a nation, Smith argues, can really only be increased by raising productivity, for example by a higher number of people in employment:

> The annual produce [...] of any nation can be increased in its value by no other means but by increasing either the number of its productive labourers or the productive powers of those labourers who had before been employed. [25]

Smith supports his argument here with the example of the three component nations of the United Kingdom – England, Scotland and Wales – which each flourished economically after customs duties between them were abolished. As an example of the consequences of not doing this he points to Germany, which, in Smith's era, still consisted of a mass of small princedoms and regional states. Thus a merchant taking his goods from Bavaria up to Prussia had to reckon, in those days, with eight different currencies and fourteen separate customs barriers – with the understandable result that trade in Germany was stagnating. That he raised so early on, then, the call for universal free trade – an ideal which seemed, in the 18th Century, impossibly distant – is one of Smith's greatest claims to the title of visionary. If we abolish all mercantilistic and protectionistic obstacles such as duties or bans on imports, while at the same time allowing anyone in any country to exercise the trade they wish – or, in other words, create a total mobility of goods and labour – this, argues Smith, will result in a fabulous degree of economic growth which will make possible prosperity, even for the least wealthy, in all nations:

It is the great multiplication of the productions of all the different arts, in consequence of the division of labour, which occasions, in a well-governed

> society, that universal opulence which extends itself to the lowest ranks of the people. [26]

To this absolute freedom of economic activity relieved of all guild and trade restrictions, customs duties, and import and export controls Smith gives the name "system of natural liberty":

> All systems, either of preference or of restraint, therefore, being thus completely taken away, the [...] system of natural liberty establishes itself of its own accord. Every man, as long as he does not violate the laws of justice, is left perfectly free to pursue his interest his own way and to bring both his industry and capital into competition with those of any other man [...]. [27]

This formulation from 1776, which urges that all individuals within a society be "left perfectly free" to practice their economic activities provided they abide by the law, remains still today the firmest and most unshakeable principle of economic liberalism.

The Free Play of Supply and Demand

This brings us to Adam Smith's central idea: the free play of supply and demand and the action of the "invisible hand". This theory of the "invisible hand" remains still today the core concept of that approach to economics which has come to dominate the Western world. Smith begins with a very simple distinction: that between natural price and market price or, as Smith prefers to call the latter, "real price". The natural price of a commodity is equal simply to the expenditures involved in producing it. These expenditures are threefold.

Firstly, the natural price is determined by expended labour-time. A product that a man has to work a week on producing naturally costs more than one he can produce in an hour. Expended labour-time was already an important factor in the hunter-and-gatherer era; in some regions the hunter who had killed a beaver could exchange it for two deer, since the labour involved in catching and killing a beaver was significantly greater. The relative difficulty of work is also a factor determining the price of its production. Thus, construction workers are granted a bad weather allowance and night-workers a hardship allowance.

A second cost-factor that any factory-owner must add into the natural price of his product consists in expenditure on the place of production or the site it stands on (e.g. rent for land, factory and warehouses).

A third such factor consists in capital investment – for example in the cotton that a manufacturer of clothing must buy from cotton-farmers as his raw material, or in the frames and looms that he needs as production machinery (and which he may have bought on credit, so that interest costs must also be added in to the natural price). There also belongs to this capital factor a reasonable profit which an entrepreneur must expect for his managerial activity, the entrepreneurial risk he takes, and the capital investment itself. Because, if he sells the clothes he makes at a price which covers just exactly the costs of production (including capital investment) and no more, he may be able to pay his workers' wages, the rent of his factory, and his raw-material costs but will have nothing left over for himself. To be added in, then, is at least a profit sufficient for him and his family to live on.

To sum up, then: the natural price of a commodity is what its maker must, at a minimum, ask for it if he is to be able to pay, in the next succeeding month, his workers, his rent, the costs of his raw materials and plant, and himself. It consists, in other words, of the costs of wages, rent, capital investment, and required profits.

Natural Price: The Price That Recoups a Sum Equal to the Total Costs of Manufacture

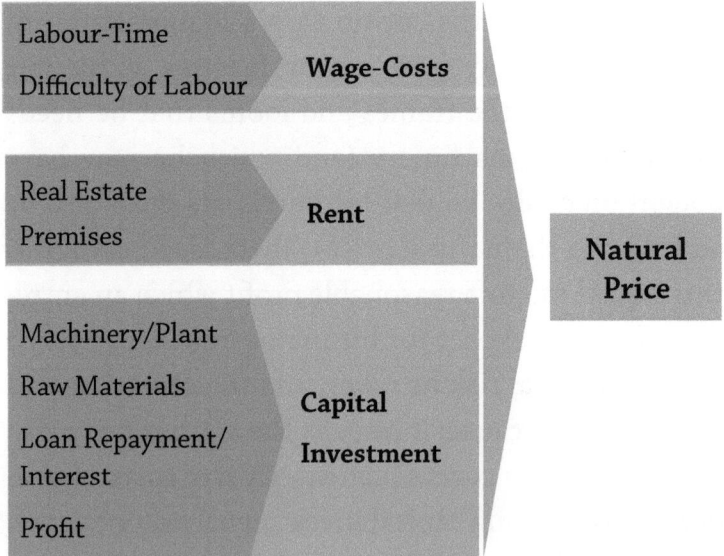

Distinct from this natural price is the real price, that is to say, the price which customers on the market are really willing to pay. Today, we would call this the market price. And this market price can deviate quite significantly from the natural price. It is determined solely and simply by relations of supply and demand.

Market Price: The Price That Buyers of the Commodity Are Really Willing to Pay

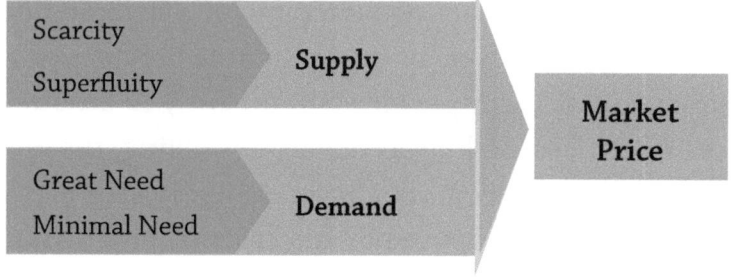

The market price can sometimes be higher, but sometimes also lower than the natural price. It is useless for an entrepreneur to insist upon charging a commodity's natural price and to explain to the customer visiting his market stall that the watch he wants to sell him cost much time and effort to make, so that he must demand its "natural price" and not a penny less if he is not to make a loss on the deal. If a similar watch is being offered more cheaply at another stall, the watchmaker will be forced to disregard this "natural price" and to sell his too for less, if he is not to be left with all his watches on his hands. The customer does not care how much time and effort has been invested in a product. He decides simply whether he wants to buy the watch at the price it is offered for or not.

The market price, then, is the actual price. But this market price can also sometimes be higher than the sum of the production costs, that is, higher than the natural price. If the manufacturer of a commodity has the good fortune of being the sole provider of a product that many people want urgently to acquire, the price rises. So long as buyers are willing, the entrepreneur can even ask a price many times greater than the sum composed by his costs of production and his previously-calculated profit – that is to say, far more than the "natural price".

In the end it is solely and simply existing demand that decides what actual price a product will fetch on the market. And yet Smith argues that the natural price of a product is the more important. Why is this? Because, Smith says, the natural price forms a kind of "centre of gravity" around which the fluctuating market price will always tend to level out. In his own words:

Smith's Central Idea

> The natural price, therefore, is, as it were, the central price, to which the prices of all commodities are continually gravitating. [28]

It does indeed sometimes happen, says Smith, that the actual price of a commodity – that is to say, its market price – rises above or falls below the level of its natural price. But this, he goes on, will always be the case only for short periods. In the longer term there exists a constant tendency for prices to gravitate toward the level of natural prices. This occurs due to the working of what Smith calls the "invisible hand".

The Invisible Hand

Smith himself chose the example, among others, of ladies' stockings to illustrate the working of the "invisible hand". But a rather more up-to-date, and possibly more perspicuous, illustration of the same principle might be drawn from that huge market in mobile telephones that has arisen only in the past few decades (even though, of course, one might use almost any product to demonstrate this formula of the "free play of supply and demand").

When they first came onto the market only a small number of companies made mobile phones. Due to the great demand it was possible to sell them at a high market price – let us say, for example, at a price of three hundred pounds a phone. Since the costs of such phones' manufacture, inclusive of all planned-in returns on investment – or, in other words, the product's "natural price" – amounted in total to only a hundred and fifty pounds, the entrepreneurs producing mobile phones in this early phase of their history were making a fat profit of one hundred and fifty pounds on each phone sold.

In the second phase of the product's history many other companies, drawn by the prospect of such high

Smith's Central Idea

profits, began also to make mobile phones. The supply of such phones increased manyfold in a short space of time and, since the demand for the product remained more or less constant, there emerged a glut of phones on the market. This in turn led to a collapse in market prices and a ruthless price war among manufacturers. Due to the glut it looked like many companies would be left with unsold phones on their hands. Finally such companies were forced, sometimes, to sell their phones at "dumping" prices that were lower than the products' costs of production, i.e. for seventy or eighty pounds or less. This meant that they were accepting a loss of seventy or eighty pounds on each phone.

The market price, in other words, dropped, in this period, below the natural price. Obviously, things could not go on long in this way, since the companies were now operating in the red and their shareholders began to protest. Many switched back, consequently, to producing other goods. Thus, in a third phase of development, the number of mobile phones produced fell once again and, since demand continued to remain constant, the market price rose once again, as a result of the new relative scarcity of supply, to the level of the natural price, and even slightly above it.

In the long run, then, it is likely that, in the following

fourth, fifth and sixth phases of the product's marketing, the market price of the phones will continue to gravitate, in such repeated wave-like motions, toward the natural price, so that finally the product costs just enough for the producer to be able, from the price received, to pay his workers, the rent on his production premises, and the costs of his plant, while getting an appropriate modest return on his own capital investment.

As soon, however, as this return begins to rise to more attractive levels, other producers are drawn once again into this sector of industry and add to the supply of the product until such a point that the market price begins to drop again. Supply and demand thus settle once again into a harmonious equilibrium. In the long term, just so many commodities are produced as the consumer has need of.

What Smith calls the "invisible hand" is nothing other than this mechanism of equilibrium. The individual entrepreneurs involved here had originally aimed at nothing but their own profit and interest. And yet they ended up doing a great service to society as a whole, without consciously intending to do so and as if guided by an "invisible hand". Their actions served to overcome the initial shortage of mobile telephones and to greatly lower the price of such

Smith's Central Idea

products; moreover, by moving into the sector of mobile telephone production they created jobs and contributed to economic growth:

> As every individual, therefore, endeavours as much as he can [...] to employ his capital [...], every individual necessarily labours to render the annual revenue of the society as great as he can. [29]

Free competition then, argues Smith, tends to result, for a nation as a whole, via the mechanism of the "invisible hand", in the most favourable possible conditions as regards supply of goods, productivity, and prices. The importance of this result is not to be underestimated. The all too "visible" hand of the planned economy repeatedly led, in many socialist states, to shortages and surpluses. For example, if planners attempted to remedy a shortage of toilet paper by decreeing an increase in the production of this commodity, this often meant that the following year there was a surplus of such paper, and consequently shortages in quite other areas.

Smith's passionate 18th-Century critique of mercantilism was taken up in the 20th Century as a critique, two hundred years *avant la lettre*, of the "planned economy" of socialism. No bureaucrat or committee of bureaucrats, Smith had argued already in 1776, could ever possibly plan the supplying of a country's population with the goods it needs, nor react so quickly to any disruptions in this supply, as can and do the thousands of entrepreneurs and tradespeople active in said country who pursue no "plan" beyond the wish to maximize their own individual profit. Under a capitalist system the shelves of shops are always filled with what the people think they stand in need of, whatever this may be.

Smith does not speak of "capitalism" but rather of "commercial society". And the secret, for Smith, of the unstoppable historical success of this "commercial society" is the transformation of the natural egoism of individual entrepreneurs into the common good of the nation as a whole. The key point is that this transformation of individual self-interest into the common good takes place, considered from the viewpoint of any individual entrepreneur, unconsciously, imperceptibly, and indeed in a manner opposed to his original selfish intention:

> He generally, indeed, neither intends to promote the public interest nor knows how much he is promoting it [...]. By directing (his) industry in such a manner as its produce may be of the greatest value, he intends only his own gain; and he is in this, as in many other cases, led by an invisible hand to promote an end which was no part of his intention. [30]

We encounter once again here, very clearly, Smith's basic assumption regarding the nature of human beings: Man is primarily inclined to pursue only his own private interests and it is only unintentionally, "led by an invisible hand", that he contributes to the wellbeing of others. It is consistent with this basic assumption that Smith expresses deep scepticism regarding all those who claim to act from altruistic motives:

> I have never known much good done by those who affected to trade for the public good. [31]

Now, Adam Smith was not only an economist but also a proponent of moral philosophy. In his first book, entitled *The Theory of the Moral Sentiments*, he shows himself entirely ready to assign to the human individual a capacity for empathy with his fellow man:

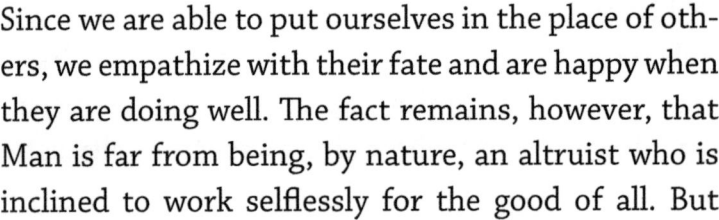

> How selfish soever Man may be supposed, there are evidently some principles in his nature which interest him in the fortune of others and render their happiness necessary to him, though he derives nothing from it except the pleasure of seeing it. [32]

Since we are able to put ourselves in the place of others, we empathize with their fate and are happy when they are doing well. The fact remains, however, that Man is far from being, by nature, an altruist who is inclined to work selflessly for the good of all. But

Smith's Central Idea

Smith does not see this as a problem. On his view, the human tendency to self-interested action suffices to hold society together. Even the greatest egoists of the British Empire, its merchants, are, Smith believes, capable of establishing a social coexistence. Because even these merchants, whose constant rapacity he acknowledges, are drawn and held together by the "invisible hand":

But [...] though among the different members of society there should be no mutual love and affection, society [...] will not necessarily be dissolved. Society may subsist among different men, as among different merchants, from a sense of its utility, without any mutual love or affection. 33

Since, in industrialized societies, people pursue highly specialized professions, and thus stand constantly in need of others in order to exchange goods and services with them, we are necessarily permanently in relation with one another – as if tied together by some invisible bond – and form a society, if for no other reason, then at least for this one:

> And though no man [in this society] should owe any obligation, or be bound in gratitude, to any other, it may still be upheld by a mercenary exchange of good offices [...]. (Beneficience) is the ornament which embellishes, not the foundation which supports, the building [...]. [34]

This foundation is and remains, rather, Man's natural striving toward the acquisition of wealth. This aspect of Man's nature cannot, Smith believes, be altered even by education. Even small children soon develop a sense of private property and try, when playing in a sandbox, to increase the number of toys under their control and to defend these toys against other children's attempts to take them away. But Smith, of course, never really gave much consideration to the question of whether and how this self-interested-

Smith's Central Idea

ness and striving toward private acquisition might be overcome, since he believed human selfishness to be already a quality of great use to society.

In the last analysis, Smith celebrates this unconsciously occurring transformation of self-interest into general social welfare as a wise and good contrivance of Nature: a kind of motor which sets mankind's activity into motion:

[...] By pursuing his own interest, (the individual) frequently promotes that of society more effectually than when he really intends to promote it. 35

Man, then, thinks, by natural inclination, only of his own advantage. But the "invisible hand" practices what Smith calls a "deception" upon Man here as regards the aim which is truly served, in the end, by each individual's actions: namely, that of promoting the general good:

> And it is well that Nature imposes upon us in this manner. It is this deception that rouses and keeps in continual motion the industry of mankind. [36]

Several decades later, a very similar construction to this was to play a central role in the philosophy of Hegel. Hegel, indeed, does not speak of the "invisible hand" but rather of the "World-Spirit" and of "the Cunning of Reason". He writes, for example, of Napoleon's having believed that he was pursuing his own interests while he was in fact, unbeknownst to himself, serving the "World-Spirit" and furthering the ends and interests of this latter. Hegel in fact describes several world-historical personalities whom he held to have been "used as instruments of the World-Spirit" in the way that Napoleon was "used", when a general in the French Revolutionary Wars, to sweep away traditional monarchies and to lay the foundations, through the introduction of the Napoleonic Code, of the modern state based solely on the rule of law. Napoleon too (so Hegel was to argue) believed to be acting out of personal ambition in doing these things; but he achieved in fact only that which served the "World-Spirit's" project of historical progress: namely, the superceding of the old feudal hierarchy by a constitutional state run by and for its citizens.

But what is the "invisible hand" in Smith's philosophy? Is it already a "World-Spirit" in Hegel's sense: a divine Reason presiding over all? Smith does speak, indeed, of a divine harmony that arises once one has established a system of natural liberty. But in the last analysis it is, for Smith, the market alone – i.e. the free play of economic forces – that ensures stability of prices, an optimal supply of goods to society, and thereby "the wealth of nations". The "invisible hand", then, cannot be understood to be, like Hegel's "World-Spirit", a metaphysical force. In Smith's philosophy, the "Cunning of Reason" consists solely in the fact that the basic egoistic instinct of the individual tends to be transformed, through the mechanism of the market, into an instrument of the general good. And just because this market mechanism of free competition is not of divine origin, it is incumbent on human beings themselves to see that it remains intact and functional:

The Duties of the State

The duty of the sovereign state, therefore, consists first and foremost in maintaining the free market and in protecting, from both internal and external dangers, a society based on the free exchange of goods:

According to the system of natural liberty the sovereign has only three duties to attend to [...] first, the duty of protecting the society from the violence and invasion of other independent societies [...]. [38]

This means maintaining a standing army, along with its commanders and a Ministry of Defence.

[...] Secondly, the duty of protecting, as far as possible, every member of the society from the injustice or oppression of every other member of it, or the duty of establishing an exact administration of justice. [...]. [39]

This means appointing judges, public prosecutors, police and prison officers whose job it is to prevent people infringing the law, taking it into their own hands, or breaching legal contracts

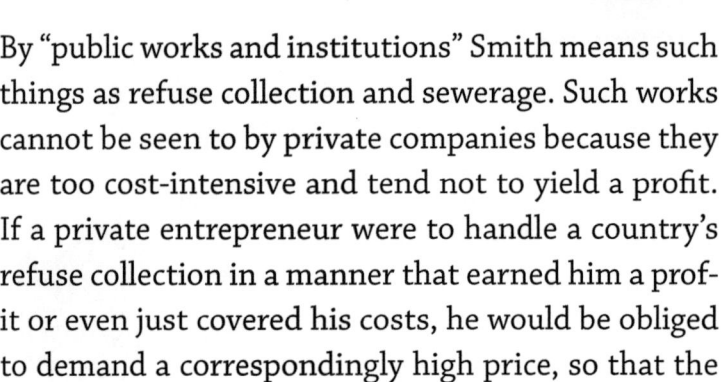

[...] And thirdly the duty of erecting and maintaining certain public works and certain public institutions which it can never be for the interest of any individual or small group of individuals to erect and maintain because the profit could never repay the expense to any individual. 40

By "public works and institutions" Smith means such things as refuse collection and sewerage. Such works cannot be seen to by private companies because they are too cost-intensive and tend not to yield a profit. If a private entrepreneur were to handle a country's refuse collection in a manner that earned him a profit or even just covered his costs, he would be obliged to demand a correspondingly high price, so that the country's citizens would be tempted to dispose of their refuse illegally. Therefore, the state itself must collect and dispose of its population's refuse at a less than commercially competitive price in order to ensure hygiene in its cities. Smith also believed that road construction ought to be a responsibility of the state, since a private entrepreneur would be obliged to demand tolls on the roads and bridges built with his private funds, another possible hindrance to trade. In Smith's view, then, some few duties still remain incumbent on the state – but only those few that cannot be performed better by a private entrepreneur. Smith warned already in 1776 against the construction of an overlarge bureaucracy which would only cost money:

The whole, or almost the whole, public revenue is, in most countries, employed in maintaining unproductive hands. [41]

Another institution which Smith believed ought to fall within the purview of the state was the school system. His call for universal compulsory education was extremely progressive for his day and age. He demanded that school attendance, as well as the attendance of adult education institutions, be free of charge. The reasons he gives for holding this to be necessary are interesting:

In the progress of the division of labour the employment of [...] the great body of the people comes to be confined to a few very simple operations, frequently to one or two. [42]

The production-line worker who spends his whole working day just setting pinheads on pins performs an activity that in no way challenges him intellectually and is thus in danger of becoming stultified:

Smith's Central Idea

> He naturally loses, therefore, the habit of (mental) exertion and generally becomes as stupid and ignorant as it is possible for a human creature to become

> [...]. But in every improved and civilized society this is the state into which [...] the great body of the people must necessarily fall, unless government takes some pains to prevent it. ⁴³

This is why Smith demands of the state that it make generous provision for the "expense of institutions for the education of youth" and "institutions for the instruction of people of all ages."⁴⁴ But for Smith the duties of the state do not extend beyond this. Beyond the employment of the necessary teachers, judges, public prosecutors, policemen, and constructors of streets, bridges and canals, he believes the bloating of the state apparatus with many officials to be an extremely harmful thing. He advocates rather a "slimmed-down" state and even warns against paying state officials too well:

> The emoluments of offices are not, like those of trades and professions, regulated by the free competition of the market [...], the persons who have the administration of government being generally disposed to reward both themselves and their immediate dependents rather more than enough. [45]

According to Smith, then, state officials should be relieved of all those tasks and functions that might possibly be able to be performed by private persons. It is the duty of the state to stay as passive as possible and to restrict itself to ensuring the good functioning of the market economy. It must leave to citizens the greatest possible space to develop their own potentialities. The state has, as it were, only the duties of a "night watchman". This phrase "night-watchman state" was coined not by Smith himself but by Ferdinand Lassalle, a critic of Smith's social philosophy who wrote about a hundred years after him. As a socialist Lassalle rejected the idea of the state's having no role extending beyond that of "night watchman"

(i.e. that of guarding against internal and external violence). He opposed to Smith's idea of a (so far as possible) passive state the idea of a socially active one: a state that would provide health insurance and pensions for its citizens and actively intervene, also in other ways, in economic life.

Taxes as an Instrument for Redistributing Wealth

In order to fund these few basic duties (i.e. national defence, law, public infrastructure and education) which he assigns to the state, Smith proposes a system of progressive taxation. This means that those who earn a higher income and achieve large profits must pay more taxes than those who earn less. Taxes are thereby, also for Smith, a regulative mechanism whereby social burdens can be fairly distributed.

Smith justifies this proposal by pointing out firstly that it is easier for the rich to pay taxes and secondly that factory-owners and traders make, in order to transport and sell their goods, a much more intensive use of the state-built roads (and indeed of the entire state-built infrastructure) than does the average working person. And in fact almost all European nations have now adopted a system of progressive taxation, scaled by income, such as Smith recommended. He recommended also, however, that governments avoid taxing higher earners, such as factory-owners, too heavily, lest they move their factories abroad:

> A merchant [...] is not necessarily the citizen of any particular country. It is in great measure indifferent to him from what place he carries on his trade. [46]

From this Smith concludes that:

> A very trifling disgust will make him remove his capital, and together with it all the industry which it supports, from one country to another. [47]

These remarks sound astonishingly far-sighted if one considers that in 1776 it was certainly no easy thing to move a company from one country to another. But Smith clearly foresees here the dangers of today's "globalization", which often results in the massive loss of jobs and of tax revenue for specific countries.

Of What Use is Smith's Discovery for Us Today?

Smith's Great Vision – Prosperity for All!

And indeed one almost gets goosebumps at the incredible exactitude with which Smith predicted future economic developments and was able to develop, some two hundred and forty years ago, precisely applicable recommendations for the present day. He foresaw, for example, that industrialization, specialization and the introduction of free trade were going to set in motion an enormous process of growth which would affect the entire national income.

Broad swathes of the populations of modern industrial societies, he foresaw, would acquire a share in prosperity – especially those he called "the labouring poor":

Of What Use is Smith's Discovery for Us Today?

> It is the great multiplication of the productions of all the different arts [...] which occasions, in a well-governed society, that universal opulence which extends itself to the lowest ranks of the people. [48]

The gross national product and the general prosperity of the population has indeed, as Smith foretold, risen exponentially in all industrialized nations in recent centuries. Today in these nations, even ordinary workers can afford to take annual holidays abroad – something quite inconceivable in Smith's day. Harold MacMillan's famous claim that ordinary people had "never had it so good" was made, indeed, in 1957 in the midst of Britain's "post-war boom". But even fifty years on, after several intervening periods of recession and crisis, his words remain true as regards people's real purchasing power. In comparison with antiquity, the Middle Ages, early modernity, or even the 19th Century – which all saw actual famine in some part or other of Western Europe – the mass of the population in industrialized countries today lives in much better material conditions than at any other time in history.

Smith's second demand too – namely, that customs duties be abolished and currencies unified so as to improve trade between the states and principalities of Europe – has now become a reality. Smith anticipated in his philosophy the present European single currency and European free trade zone. Smith's vision extended, however, to a system of free trade in which all countries would take part, agreeing together to renounce all customs duties. Even this vision is now, two hundred and forty years after Smith's writing, almost a reality. Today, the World Trade Organization sees to it that the rules of global free trade are observed.

Admittedly, the unrestricted global economic activity that now goes under the name "globalization" is proving, contrary to the optimism about free trade expressed by Smith, to be a serious destabilizing factor. Many jobs once performed in industrialized nations are now being, or might soon be, moved to low-wage countries. Such long-industrialized countries as Britain, Germany, France, Italy, Russia and the USA are already suffering the consequences of global competition from Eastern Europe, China, Korea and other regions on the economic rise.

But Smith teaches us an important lesson precisely in this regard. Free trade – and the "globalization" that it brings – lead in fact to a convergence of living conditions. Because prosperity is nothing fixed and firm which a nation can secure for itself once and for all in the form of gold, raw materials or territory. Rather, prosperity is to be found wherever there is what Smith calls "industry" (meaning not established material facilities but rather the industriousness that animates these things). Not acquired possessions, but rather the continuing development of productive energy, is what is decisive, in the end, for "the wealth of nations":

> The annual produce [...] of any nation can be increased in its value by no other means but by increasing either the number of its productive labourers or the productive powers of those labourers who had before been employed. [49]

It is characteristic of capitalism, says Smith, that capitalist production will always be carried on wherever it is cheapest to do so – that is, wherever wages are lowest and people enjoy least prosperity. But once production has been shifted to such regions, purchasing power, prices and wages automatically rise there too. Thus, through globalized production, prosperity comes also to those countries that had hitherto had no part in it. But to lament this would be, on Smith's principles, a very short-sighted way of looking at things. Because this improvement in living conditions and progressive interpenetration of the economies of all nations serves to secure social peace in the long term and to remove breeding grounds for nationalism. Those countries, for example, which are integrated into the European economic and currency union no longer go to war against one another and apply common standards of law. Thus France and Germany overcame a hereditary enmity that had lasted centuries by joining together in a cooperation on coal and steel production from which there later grew the economic and currency union of the EU. As Smith had foretold, they grew together socially and economically.

The same applies – viewed over a longer time-period – worldwide. In view of his liberal call for the free unfolding of economic activity, Smith would surely also have welcomed present developments in Asia. We see, for example, an extremely rapid growth in prosperity and quality of life today for all the people of China. Thanks to the increasing transfer of goods manufacture into emergent countries we might well see, in the long term, a global rapprochement of living conditions. And just this was Adam Smith's great vision: a worldwide raising of living standards within a system of natural liberty – the "wealth of nations". Smith, then, was anything but a nationalist or a narrow patriot. As both economist and cosmopolitan, he placed his hopes in the dynamic, and in the binding force, of the global economy. Perhaps we too will now succeed in understanding the tremendous dynamic of globalization no longer just as a threat but as also, following Smith, an opportunity – an opportunity for a global economic merging of mankind.

The System of Natural Liberty – Smith's Warning Against the Planned Economy

In the end, Smith argued, the free exchange of goods and free competition on all markets will give rise to global prosperity. And this self-regulating system of a market economy will, once it has developed, prove far superior to any economic policy guided by the "planned economy" model. In a market economy, disparities in income themselves become important positive incentives:

> It is the interest of every man to live as much at his ease as he can; and if his emoluments are to be precisely the same whether he does or does not perform some very laborious duty, it is certainly his interest [...] to neglect (such duties) altogether. [50]

Of What Use is Smith's Discovery for Us Today?

Smith expresses here – eighty years before the Communist Manifesto and a hundred and thirty years before the Russian Revolution – the worst imaginable prognosis for the socialist experiment.

Smith's warning words gain great force when one looks back on the actual history of states like the Soviet Union, where the crops of the huge collective farms were often mediocre at best, while the peasants who had been forced to collectivize continued to grow good and copious produce in the tiny family allotments that collectivization allowed them to retain, selling this produce at local markets to get by. In the long term, the planned economies of the socialist states could not keep pace with rival market economies. Production and living standards stagnated and the worldwide triumph of capitalism was assured.

After the general global collapse of the planned economy and the collectivist model of society Smith seems indeed to have been proven right in his view that individuals, if they are to be truly productive, must be granted room to pursue their self-interest:

> If he is naturally active and a lover of labour, it is his interest to employ that activity in any way from which he can derive some advantage, rather than in the performance of his duty, from which he can derive none. [51]

Smith was not criticizing here, of course, the planned economy of the socialist states, which were founded only long after his day, but rather the "mercantilists", who foreshadowed socialist planning with their attempts to guide and control exports, imports, and domestic production by state intervention and state-sponsored enterprises. Smith was sure that state functionaries could never plan and produce the goods needed and desired by a nation as perfectly as could this nation's competing entrepreneurs and tradesmen, with their instinct for profit. He had a general mistrust of every sort of state planning, by politicians, of economic life:

Of What Use is Smith's Discovery for Us Today?

> The man of system [...] seems to imagine that he can arrange the different members of a great society with as much ease as the hand arranges the different pieces upon a chess-board. He does not consider [...] that in the great chess-board of human society every single piece has a principle of motion of its own [...]. [52]

And this "principle of motion of its own" possessed by "each piece on the social chess-board" – i.e. each individual's natural inclination to improve his or her own situation – can only develop within a "system of natural liberty", i.e. within a free market economy. If each individual is just allowed to use his or her own powers in their own personal interest, they will contribute thereby – without intending to do so and guided by an "invisible hand" – to the good of all. Smith expresses here an idea which was to remain for subsequent centuries, right up to the present day, the central idea of the free market economy:

> In general, if any branch of trade, or any division of labour, be advantageous to the public, the freer and more general the competition, it will always be the more so. [53]

There can be no doubt but that Smith, with his theory of the "invisible hand", established the basic principle explaining and justifying the action of the market economy and predicted, with uncanny accuracy, later economic developments. But in the course of recent history a dark shadow has been cast also over this action of the "invisible hand". The free play of supply and demand did not in fact always function so smoothly and harmoniously as Smith had thought it would. In the 1930s, for example – something that Smith had certainly not foreseen – the industrialized countries suffered an economic catastrophe of unprecedented scale: the Great Depression. Did the "invisible hand" fail here in its essential function?

Global Economic Crises – the End of the 'Invisible Hand'?

On "Black Tuesday" in 1929 the New York Stock Exchange crashed. There followed a long period of worldwide mass unemployment and a massive driving down of wages for those in work. The "invisible hand", the free play of economic forces, broke down. Productivity stagnated; many firms cut back and dismissed workers; wages fell without an end in sight. For Smith, the very idea of a wage implies an inherent lower limit:

> A man must always live by his work, and his wages must at least be sufficient to maintain him. They must even upon most occasions be somewhat more; otherwise it would be impossible to bring up a family and the race of such workers could not last beyond the first generation. [54]

Wages, then, cannot fall below the minimum needed for subsistence, or at least not for long:

> [...] There is [...] a certain rate below which it seems impossible to reduce, for any considerable time, the ordinary wages even of the lowest species of labour. 55

Another reason, Smith argues, why wages can only for very short periods fall below the minimum needed for subsistence is that the action of supply and demand will see to it that they soon rise again:

> If the reward (of labour) should at any time be less than what was requisite for the purpose (of ensuring a steady labour supply), the deficiency of hands would soon raise it. 56

Wages fall, argues Smith, only until a point is reached where the supply of labour has become, due to emigration and decrease in population, so scarce that the market itself forces the entrepreneur to pay higher wages once again if he is to find anyone to work for him. In Smith's day, the unemployed and poor day-labourers and farm workers did indeed often emigrate to America to try their luck in the New World. But during the Great Depression this was no longer possible since America itself was affected.

Another hope and belief of Smith's that history did not bear out was the idea that the continuing economic growth of the industrial nations would lead also to an ever-growing demand for workers. Since Smith's day capitalism's growth has in fact been constantly interrupted by dramatic phases of stagnation and recession. During the ten long years of the Great Depression there appeared even to be being fulfilled all the prophecies of Smith's great critic Karl Marx. Due to the flood of bankruptcies and mass lay-offs the purchasing power of the population fell dramatically and those firms that were still producing were unable to sell their goods. They continued to produce for a while, until their warehouses were full, but then had to begin laying off workers themselves, since they could no longer pay their wages. This meant that still fewer goods were bought so that the whole economic system ground to a halt. Automation also destroyed many jobs, since a few machines now took over the production tasks once performed by thousands of workers, resulting in long-term unemployment and poverty. In some European countries this led to a political radicalization of the population. The impoverished masses and the frightened middle classes voted in fascist regimes, dooming humanity to a Second World War. But even after the war the tendency of unemployment rates to reach menacing levels during recessions has remained, right up to today, an unresolved problem of the market economy.

It was for this reason that economists – John Maynard Keynes first among them – began to argue against reliance solely on Smith's "invisible hand" and on the self-regulation of the economy. The state, argued Keynes and others, should not just look on and be "night-watchman" to the market but needed, in times of crisis, to itself intervene actively in the processes of the market economy. Keynes even advocated a so-called "counter-cyclical" fiscal policy in certain economic situations. The state, Keynes argued, should, at times when the economy is strong – i.e. times of low unemployment and high productivity – use tax increases to draw money out of circulation, so as to avoid the economy's "overheating". This money can then, in times of recession and high unemployment, be pumped back into economic circulation. The state can use the money thus placed at its disposal to counter the stagnation typical of crises by awarding, for example, in such recessionary periods, large construction firms contracts to build new roads. This artificial stimulation of a temporarily stagnant economy, extended to as many sectors as possible, would, Keynes argued, serve to lower unemployment. And with more people in work, purchasing power would increase and the cycle of healthy economic activity once again be set in motion.

And in fact, since the Great Depression, many governments have implemented such "counter-cyclical" measures in crisis periods. But many politicians and economic policy-makers remain nonetheless advocates of Adam Smith's doctrines in their purest form and demand that – even in, indeed particularly in, crisis periods – trust must be maintained in the economy's power to heal itself, that is, in the "invisible hand" and the laws of supply and demand. These neo-liberal politicians and economists consider it to be merely a natural and healthy "market adjustment" when certain firms, discovering that they have overproduced their goods and that the market is over-supplied with them, fail and go bankrupt. Government subsidies and "counter-cyclical" measures taken in such a situation represent, according to the diehard advocates of Adam Smith, artificial, useless and even harmful interventions, because such non-viable firms were bound to drop out of economic competition sooner or later anyway. Better for all to let things take their course, say these neo-liberal economist policy-makers, arguing that what proves unviable on the market cannot be artificially maintained by the taxpayer.

This discussion about when the state should intervene and when it should abide by Smith's recommendations and abstain from all intervention in the market continues today with no end in sight. Even trans-national European authorities are sometimes divided on such questions as whether a government should give subsidies to a large firm in difficulties or whether this should be forbidden as a distortion of fair competition. The European Union does in fact often forbid its member states to "bail out" large private enterprises with taxpayers' money, in order to ensure free and fair competition as this was understood by Smith. We see here what a live and present issue Smith's call for a "system of natural liberty" remains. Despite the arguments made by Keynes and

Keynesians for active state intervention in times of economic difficulty, European economic policies still tend to wager principally on the power of free competition. European state governments make, indeed, minor interventions in crisis periods but stay, for the most part, economically passive. Moreover, since states now run very high national debts, the money is often lacking for such interventions. In other words, nations continue, in large part, to rely on the "invisible hand".

From "Night-Watchman State" to "Welfare State" – The Legacy of Adam Smith

Smith's teachings, of course, have been developed and adapted over the years. Thus, the German professor Walther Eucken criticized Smith for his having completely forgotten to protect his "free competition" from monopolies and price-rigging. Whereas Smith had mistrusted every state intervention, Eucken pointed out that the state needed to intervene with antitrust and anti-monopoly measures in order to prevent the market's being overly dominated by certain economic agents. Eucken rightly pointed out that "competition is a state institution." He called his own economic model "ordoliberalism". Smith himself, indeed, had strongly argued, in his day, against "monopolies" but he had been thinking primarily of state monopolies. He did not foresee the need for anti-cartel legislation.

It was perhaps Eucken's native country, Germany, along with the Scandinavian nations, that provided the most striking proof, during the latter half of the 20th Century, of how Smith's economic principles could be both adopted and supplemented, creating socio-economic systems which proved, surprisingly, able to combine the free market forces that Smith had embraced with the state guidance and control he had rejected. In Germany, this supplemented free-market economic system was called the "social market economy" and it was within such a framework that Germany achieved its impressive "Economic Miracle" in the years after WW2. But, under a range of other names, this "ordoliberal" social market economy became, in fact, in the last half of the 20th Century, almost a worldwide social norm. The Labour government elected in Britain in 1945 implemented most of the far-reaching measures regarding state-supported health, unemployment, and retirement insurance that had been worked out before and during the war by the economist and civil servant William Beveridge. And even in the United States, traditionally the land of "rugged independence", the Democratic Party administrations which dominated the decade of the 1960s developed – above all under the banner of Lyndon Johnson's "Great Society" agenda – the structures of an enduring welfare state and actively pursued a programme of state-led redistribution of wealth.

For all the talk, in more recent decades, of a steady dismantlement of the welfare state and of a global return to free-market capitalism in its purest and most unconditional form, this goal of preserving, in its essence, Smith's "free play of market forces" but supplementing it with state interventions and redistributive programmes remains a guiding ideal for many nations worldwide. There is a broad global consensus today that the state should provide protection from poverty and misery to low-earners, the unemployed, children, the aged and the sick, financing this protection of the needy from taxes and other contributions. Smith, indeed, had advocated a system of progressive taxation whereby rich people paid more than poor; but he was far from assigning to the state real duties of wealth-redistribution. Much more than this has come to be expected from the modern state. Adam Smith's "night-watchman state" has largely made way for the "welfare state". Nonetheless, there can be no doubt that Smith did lay, with his concept of a free market economy, the foundations for modern society.

Thus, the members of the Mont Pelerin Society – a regularly meeting global association of eminent sociologists, economists and politicians who stand close to economic liberalism but who include not just neoliberals but proponents of ordoliberalism and the social market economy – still proudly wear the "Adam Smith tie" so as to show their intellectual affinity with the forefather of the free market economy.

Adam Smith had the great vision that, through the division of labour, the removing of all guild restraints and the abolition of customs duties and barriers, a worldwide trade would arise which would bind all nations together and lead to prosperity for all. Today there still exist, globally, a great "North-South" divide and, within the nations, significant differences in wealth. But there has inarguably been achieved, in the centuries since Smith, a perceptible improvement in living standards and life expectancy for large swathes of the population.

Smith's hope of an ever-increasing prosperity of all citizens was inspired by the simple but fascinating idea that technical progress and specialization have placed human beings, for the first time in the history of our species, in a position where we produce significantly more things than we can ourselves use. Since this applies generally, in the modern world, to all individuals, there has grown up a system of the exchange of good for good, extending to every type of commodity and on a scale never seen before, that has brought about a massive enrichment of the life of modern Man:

> Each (person) supplies (other people) abundantly with what they have occasion for, and they accommodate him as amply with what he has occasion for, and a general plenty diffuses itself through all the different ranks of society. [57]

Bibliographical References:

1. Adam Smith, The Wealth of Nations, Books I-III, edited and with an introduction by Andrew Skinner, Penguin Books, London, 1999, p. 119
2. Adam Smith, The Wealth of Nations, Books IV-V, edited and with an introduction by Andrew Skinner, Penguin Books, London, 1999, p. 32
3. Adam Smith, The Wealth of Nations, Books I-III, edited and with an introduction by Andrew Skinner, Penguin Books, London, 1999, p. 429
4. Ibid. p. 115
5. Joseph A. Schumpeter, History of Economic Analysis, Routledge Publishers, 1986, p. 176
6. Adam Smith, The Wealth of Nations, Books I-III, edited and with an introduction by Andrew Skinner, Penguin Books, London, 1999, p. 441
7. Adam Smith, The Theory of the Moral Sentiments, edited by D. D. Raphael and A. L. Macfie, Oxford University Press, 1976, p. 183
8. Ibid.
9. Adam Smith, The Wealth of Nations, Books IV-V, edited and with an introduction by Andrew Skinner, Penguin Books, London, 1999, p. 298
10. Adam Smith, The Wealth of Nations, Books I-III, edited and with an introduction by Andrew Skinner, Penguin Books, London, 1999, p. 488-9
11. Adam Smith, The Wealth of Nations, Books IV-V, edited and with an introduction by Andrew Skinner, Penguin Books, London, 1999, p. 298
12. Ibid.
13. Adam Smith, The Wealth of Nations, Books I-III, edited and with an introduction by Andrew Skinner, Penguin Books, London, 1999, p. 225
14. Adam Smith, The Wealth of Nations, Books I-III, edited and with an introduction by Andrew Skinner, Penguin Books, London, 1999, pps. 109-110

15 Ibid.
16 Ibid.
17 Ibid. p. 118
18 Ibid.
19 Ibid. p. 119
20 Adam Smith, The Wealth of Nations, Books IV-V, edited and with an introduction by Andrew Skinner, Penguin Books, London, 1999, p. 33
21 Ibid.
22 Ibid.
23 Adam Smith, The Wealth of Nations, Books IV-V edited and with an introduction by Andrew Skinner, Penguin Books, London, 1999, pps. 15-16
24 Adam Smith, The Wealth of Nations, Books IV-V edited and with an introduction by Andrew Skinner, Penguin Books, London, 1999, pps. 16-17
25 Adam Smith, The Wealth of Nations, Books I-III, edited and with an introduction by Andrew Skinner, Penguin Books, London, 1999, p. 443
26 Ibid. p. 115
27 Adam Smith, The Wealth of Nations, Books IV-V edited and with an introduction by Andrew Skinner, Penguin Books, London, 1999, pps. 273-4
28 Adam Smith, The Wealth of Nations, Books I-III, edited and with an introduction by Andrew Skinner, Penguin Books, London, 1999, p. 160
29 Adam Smith, The Wealth of Nations, Books IV-V edited and with an introduction by Andrew Skinner, Penguin Books, London, 1999, p. 32
30 Ibid.
31 Ibid.
32 Adam Smith, The Theory of the Moral Sentiments, edited by D. D. Raphael and A. L. Macfie, Oxford University Press, 1976, p. 9
33 Ibid. p. 86
34 Ibid.
35 Adam Smith, The Wealth of Nations, Books IV-V edited and with an introduction by Andrew Skinner, Penguin Books, London, 1999, p. 32

36 Adam Smith, The Theory of the Moral Sentiments, edited by D. D. Raphael and A. L. Macfie, Oxford University Press, 1976, p. 183
37 Adam Smith, The Wealth of Nations, Books I-III, edited and with an introduction by Andrew Skinner, Penguin Books, London, 1999, p. 429.
38 Adam Smith, The Wealth of Nations, Books IV-V, edited and with an introduction by Andrew Skinner, Penguin Books, London, 1999, p. 274
39 Ibid.
40 Ibid.
41 Adam Smith, The Wealth of Nations, Books I-III, edited and with an introduction by Andrew Skinner, Penguin Books, London, 1999, p. 442
42 Adam Smith, The Wealth of Nations, Books IV-V edited and with an introduction by Andrew Skinner, Penguin Books, London, 1999, p. 368
43 Ibid. pps. 368-9
44 Ibid. p. 348 and p. 375
45 Adam Smith, The Wealth of Nations, Books IV-V edited and with an introduction by Andrew Skinner, Penguin Books, London, 1999, p. 461
46 Adam Smith, The Wealth of Nations, Books I-III, edited and with an introduction by Andrew Skinner, Penguin Books, London, 1999, p. 519
47 Ibid.
48 Ibid. p. 115
49 Ibid. p. 443
50 Adam Smith, The Wealth of Nations, Books IV-V edited and with an introduction by Andrew Skinner, Penguin Books, London, 1999, pps. 349-50
51 Ibid. p. 350
52 Adam Smith, The Theory of the Moral Sentiments, edited by D. D. Raphael and A. L. Macfie, Oxford University Press, 1976, p. 234
53 Adam Smith, The Wealth of Nations, Books I-III, edited and with an introduction by Andrew Skinner, Penguin Books, London, 1999, p. 429

54 Ibid. p. 170
55 Ibid.
56 Ibid. p. 183
57 Ibid. p. 115

Already published in the same series:

Walther Ziegler
Camus in 60 Minutes
ISBN 9783741227738

Walther Ziegler
Freud in 60 Minutes
ISBN 9783741227707

Walther Ziegler
Hegel in 60 Minutes
ISBN 9783741227677

Walther Ziegler
Heidegger in 60 Minutes
ISBN 9783741227752

Walther Ziegler
Kant in 60 Minutes
ISBN 9783741226373

Walther Ziegler
Marx in 60 Minutes
ISBN 9783741227691

Walther Ziegler
Platon in 60 Minutes
ISBN 9783741227615

Walther Ziegler
Rousseau in 60 Minutes
ISBN 9783741227622

Walther Ziegler
Sartre in 60 Minutes
ISBN 9783741227653

Walther Ziegler
Smith in 60 Minutes
ISBN 9783741227721

Coming soon in the same series:

Walther Ziegler
Adorno in 60 Minutes

Walther Ziegler
Arendt in 60 Minutes

Walther Ziegler
Bacon in 60 Minutes

Walther Ziegler
Descartes in 60 Minutes

Walther Ziegler
Foucault in 60 Minutes

Walther Ziegler
Habermas in 60 Minutes

Walther Ziegler
Hobbes in 60 Minutes

Walther Ziegler
Nietzsche in 60 Minutes

Walther Ziegler
Popper in 60 Minutes

Walther Ziegler
Rawls in 60 Minutes

Walther Ziegler
Schopenhauer in 60 Minutes

Walther Ziegler
Wittgenstein in 60 Minutes

The author:

Dr Walther Ziegler is academically trained in the fields of philosophy, history and political science. As a foreign correspondent, reporter and newsroom coordinator for the German TV station ProSieben he has produced films on every continent. His news reports have won several prizes and awards. He has also authored numerous books in the field of philosophy. His many years of experience as a journalist mean that he is able to present the complex ideas of the great philosophers in a way that is both engaging and very clear. Since 2007 he has also been active as a teacher and trainer of young TV journalists in Munich, holding the post of Academic Director at the Media Academy, an institute of higher education that offers film and TV courses at its base directly on the site of the major European film production company Bavaria Film.